BLUE OBLIVION

THE TASTE OF CHROME

Written by Alex Fatouros

The Taste of Chrome © 2011 Alex Fatouros

LEO FATOUROS 12.2.22 – 25.4.98

Blue Oblivion

Layout and design by Andrew Fatouros.

This is the First Edition of The Taste Of Chrome

ISBN 978-0-646-55329-0

This book is dedicated to my family. . .

. . . Blood in blood out . . .

Thanks: Peter, Maree, Andrew, Joyce,
John Meehan, David Walsh, Kahmal Haddad,
Andrew Demchyshyn, Meredith Laval,
Matthew Tagkalidis, Jeremy ('The Guru').

See, the name of the LORD
　　　　comes from far away,
　　　burning with his anger, and in
　　　rising smoke;
his lips are full of indignation,
　　　and his tongue is like
　　　　a devouring fire;
his breathe is like an overflowing
　　　stream
　　　that reaches up to the neck –
to sift the nations with the sieve
　　　of destruction,
　　　and to place on the jaws of the
　　　　peoples a bridle that leads
　　　　them astray.

- ISIAH 27.28

CONTENTS

PORT OF ENTRY

In a codeine dream these streets become a vast,
playground of slanting traffic lights and sex-crazed
office workers

Who at five in the afternoon,
keep their dreams hidden, of chaos moving . . .
through trapped lungs and fragile glass breaking.

So much pressure kept under a city's walls . . . in sewers,
drain pipes and the shattered illusions of peace.

We work to keep our nightmares clean
thin of the legions of liars, and the
working class torture.

At night we dance to a new morning glory.
Where at once we are reborn and the new dawn
enters . . . where we fight to keep ourselves pure . . .
on the inside,

Away from their selected diseases . . .

ABSTRACT

Sometimes you strike a chord with humanity
and it is reassuring to know
that in a few moments time they will probably hate you,
but in these days of preoccupied stupidity
it is highly appropriate to cast down
the ones you used to love.

I, of all people know that insanity is just one trip,
the trip that lasts too long in the fire
and at the same time . . . soaks the pages of all your journals,
while I'm in the hallway pissing . . . pretending,
to be the one on the walls with Jesus.

CATHOLIC BOY
-For Jim Carroll

Tiny soldiers form shadows
against the backs of my eyelids
each day a priest dies in your
dreams, and you tear pages,
from childrens encyclopedias.
In the morning you wake to find pine
needles scattered across your bed
my sister fell and died yesterday
from the second story of my brothers
apartment. Malcolm my best friend
died just over a year ago when
a train hit his body and left him stabbed at
the side of the tracks; his left wrist scarred
and broken like that little girl who was abducted
on the news channel. Eight is the channel
of the news, a good number say the Chinese
my father built me a paper boat and we
sailed it down the river until we found ourselves
a model plane and I suppose planes are better
than boats as both contain feelings
of nostalgia . . . however the planes go
faster and you get to *leave* quicker
how are you in the evenings?

Two people. A man and a woman making

love beside the tracks of a train where they
found my best friend Malcolm in the morning.
And they have no idea about the paper boat
I made with my father yet somehow they are on it.

LONELY, CHEAP NIGHT

Through bars, porno theatres and alley ways –
through motels where the rich people fuck . . .
each night calling it love . . .
Through slums of the city, and
the madhouses of the State, the gambling houses, the drunk
houses. With dying men and women, and old wasted friends,
drinking themselves into the slowest, forms of suicide . . .
Slaughtering their minds and bodies
For addiction's sake . . .
In some psychiatric ward . . .
In some nuthouse seclusion room
In some rehab centre.
Always remember that they were still human . . .
That anyone can lose it – at anytime . . .
Can become a drunk, a heroin addict, a murderer,
or simply a slave . . .
Men and women, continually
Locked up for seeing things askew.
In a seclusion room for their own sly methods of escape
And trying to speak out of turn
Or worse, a straight jacket
Forcing you to stay glued to your own worst nightmares
That play on the walls as the blood drips slowly down
As your world tastes like rotting toy train sets,
On fire in your mouth –
Words from the illusion, scattered on old mattresses . . .
Words that flicker against the cold off-white cellars of the night

And that night, rages on, always a lonely night . . .
Nothing ceases, to ease up on you –
And forced to listen to some fucked up doctors
Description of sanity . . .
And how you remain foreign to it
As they strangle themselves and mutilate themselves,
And chew off pieces of thickened meat -
From their own tongues . . .

Writing poetry with their own shit
against blood and piss stained walls
It's a lonely night, in the city tonight,
The whores walk past you . . .
As they think of greed
I sit here and think of lust . . .
I wonder how the two emotions . . .
Correlate w/one another
Then I remember to think:
          'Hey dumb arse, you/re still out here
drifting . . . all alone, in the lonely,
cheap night. Red neon flashing, all around you,
while you sit there wishing it were
blue… but it isn't.'
          So the best thing to do would be to
Walk away . . .
Think for a little while longer
Then maybe go grab a steak sandwich,
Medium & bloody

Then catch a show at the city triple XXX parlour
Because what else have you got to do?
But admit to yourself:

'I am one of the lonely, cheap night.'

INSANITY

It has followed me through
hospital hallways, whore houses,
bars, streets of isolation, motels, and
many other places, for more
than eleven years . . .

Insanity . . .
carved into my mind and soul
like fire,
like torture,
like the useless screams of some
rape victim in a nameless
street.

Like the pointless mutilation
   of some lonely, begging, soldier. . .
         Insanity,
like the child of twelve,
   getting dragged through a cellar – to her rape &
     murder. . .

. . . as the water collects
in the basement of your own private

hell. . .

Like bad acid.

Like insanity.

Like the cut-off ear of an unknown painter.

The mind of some young mother
as she attempts to abort
the unborn fetus   dwelling up inside her

in a subway toilet
from shooting a filthy syringe
up into her

snatch.

Like the Roman soldier who drives the last nails
into J C's hands and feet.

Like the bloody virgins of faith,
With a veil never lifting.

Like the scarred woman who has had acid poured all over her
face. And why in the name of Christ, does this shit, continue to
happen?

Madness.

Like when the eyes

are scratched to shit by the
dirty whore's on Smith Street.

The insanity that rips into
your guts
and, leaves you feeling like the only thing,
you have left
in this world
is a useless scream
that nobody cares to
hear.

A madness of poverty.
A poverty of madness.

Insanity, incest, murder,
genocide,
civil war, world war,
Famine,
Apocalypse,
Etc, etc…
Madness of a slaves last words
drowning out into his absolute

Silence.

SOLITUDE (It Isn't The Worst Of Things . . .)

I sit alone on another Friday night.
There is little left to do now.
I have just finished,
jerking off to some cheap
porno magazine, and
now I feel even more hollow . . .
than I was before –
even more unsatisfied . . .
enough to give me
something
to write this
poem
about.
And there is that pathetic kind of feeling.
That the only time you feel
you have
something
worthy enough to say,
is when you feel totally
empty.
Alone.
By yourself.
Hollow.
In solitude.
There is nothing here now.
      Thinking, of myself

like this, forever, slowly
ageing.

       Slow
Death
            Patterns
      of a morbid cycle.

Feeling it like this, then
writing it all down on this
page. It gets you there,
this struggle to reach some kind of
purity,
in the form of words
it helps you
feel less alone.
It creeps up
on you, however, that
feeling
that you can no longer, bring
yourself to an easy
smile. It takes a lot of hard
work now. To smile . . . kind of like
you have to force it.
And there is this fear there inside that you
might learn to grow comfortable
with the mask, with the pain;
that you may forget how to really

be yourself. And if you let this happen
then everything else will slowly turn
to shit. I know this.

It is not much
to write these bullshit poems
late at night. In complete isolation,
apart from the *Patti Smith* record playing
on my record machine. Writing, it all down
in the early hours of, what has now become, Saturday
morning. Slowly the lines extend, and you start
to feel better. You breathe more easily, more
freely now. And yeah, hell, I know, they aren't much at all, these poems
but writing them is a process that sheds a little light –
   and for every futile attempt I make
      to write the words
     that are slowly forming in my mind
      I break out of the cycle a little bit
of slow death
perpetually
forming…

        And I feel a little bit of the

  Light.

     That will not let me give in.

IT HITS YOU LIKE A MOTHERFUCKING FIST

It hits you like a motherfucking fist,
real words – they, almost reach inside your guts
and tear
chunks away –

Yeah, it hits you hard –
like a Saigon whore's grip around your ball-sack
at least this is what my
uncle tells me . . . A return soldier . . . from that Hell in Vietnam.

Listening to Iggy Pop scream '*Dirt*',
a song from the *Funhouse* album.

I should've been a few years older, w/
better eyesight . . . could've gone to Nam and killed
a couple of VC guys, maybe then my fucking insanity would
have made some sense to me . . .

Yeah, it hits you hard, like a motherfucking fist, real words,
poetry.

Not this.

#6

- For Mary

I traced the lines of total fear -
this morning. Awoke on the edges
of a bed, where my virginity
had been misplaced.

A whore smiled at me and said:
'You do not have to fold the dirty towels'.

THE SUBTERRANEAN LOVE

- For Her Memory

In a tortured dream
soft blood melts my voice tremors . . .
I still shake . . .
fear drops out of my body
tangled angel hair, greased with cancer
left handed girl . . . sticks a pin inside her vein
the poems
breaking loose, they are always coming
like breaking waves loose in my head
As I sail through black swamps of the mind,
dreaming . . . the TV is shot with noise,
like funk music pumping through me,
the edges of her needle . . . her eyes, so slanted,
but only with hatred.

And when I think about it,
I can only see, the falling blood
The ashes turning the water . . .
To lead. Like a weight. A stone,
a child crying in the name of love . . .

The movie plays through me –
As I come in and out of the nightmare.

It was a dream poisoned by a youth,

displaced.

I am just trying to maintain
my sanity.

I wanted to offer you . . . everything,
All of my love…
All of my surrender . . .
All of my dying visions
The movie played – and the cars
Were frozen chrome . . .
As I tripped out on the metallic host,
And listened to the saxophones;
Of a jazz band in the deadened night -
Where Satan played like Coltrane –
Coming down from the trip . . .

Broken windows to the cathedrals
of the cheap lurid nightscapes
I should've entered when I got the chance . . .
I should've held on stronger
Tried to escape
The poisoned reversal
Of a piped up false mythology
                      . . . . but you can't always end up
              thinking like this . . .

when the coin burns in your mouth

like cancer . . .

or an unknown calling . . .

         . . . I should have just forced myself to commit

            the hatred. . . of images

those such as the broken carnival swings – rusted and dirty

and sealed with blood

they swung, in the circus

of our own hell . . .

and they broke the eardrums,

and pain slit the throats of opium drained patients . . .

     . . . and now it might have been so different . . .

     if by night the soccer field had been empty,

as the pitcher's they drank, in bars, and blackened cancer

hadn't been so cruel - as it was to you . . .

like the ritualized conceptions of

the babies that fed on jaundiced milk,

here in this, place . . . everything feeds on

life . . . steals it by the meter . . .

(we choke to enter –

we must choke to leave)

What God, created this cruel, irony of pain?

There is no escaping the piped up dreams/nightmares,
Or fractured mythologies . . .

Only the vanishing illusions –
and the sterling silver pins
which they stuck to your flesh, and your blood-curdling screams,
couldn't break the prisons of your mental agony
seeping through the night. . . like welting wax,
which drips into a dead dog's bloodshot eyes. . .
And the words ceiling wax could've sounded poetic. . .
In a different atmosphere . . .

Sending me back. . . to blindness. . .
        again. . .

        Time after time . . .

        We'll still be here. . .

. . . to bask in your memory...

R.I.P. (A Soldiers Eulogy)

- For Leo Fatouros

He left his home and family
At the age of sixteen.

He was a young man unprepared for the horrors
the war would bring.

His father grappled for money in the auditoriums,
Years earlier. They had said he accidently killed a man,
after the guy broke into his house…
his father knocked the guy down a flight of stairs
with a single punch.
They always said he had hands like watermelons.
And he taught his son the art of the take-down,
on Sundays;
as the two of them would grapple and fight –
wrestling on the floors of the living room. Where they put
countless holes
      into the walls…
The young man's sister, Isabelle
screamed that they were going to brake something else.

So the young man went to war…
And at the age of eighteen became a sergeant.

Taught unarmed combat to the other soldiers.

He was good with his hands…
Had a practical mind, as well as
an imaginative one.

So they had him fixing tanks…
When there were little or no spare parts (I guess,
the imagination, he had, helped him with this).

He was the only guy in his battalion who had a machine gun.

There was a particular day
when one of the troops in his battalion
Shot a Japanese man in the head…
Blood ran
from his body like diseased oil spewing out
of a punctured oil tank…
He was an informer, for the Americans.
But I guess, that shit doesn't ease you any,
when a Jap soldier has just killed your best buddy…an hour
earlier.

So the leader of this battalion, deciding
to do something 'practical', took, his friends gun, and swapped it
with his own…

He took the chance that when the lieutenant searched their rifles
He wouldn't have thought the sergeant would have killed this
dead soldier…

They didn't search his rifle.

He went crazy, trying to fix tanks without parts.
So they locked him up in a make shift mental hospital.
Straight-jacketed him and knocked him out to shave...
Wouldn't let him piss, when he needed to.

Is this how the sick are supposed to be treated?

Is this what our wars are doing to good men?
And what about the wives, and the children of those left behind?

Later on he got lost in the jungles of Bougainville –
Threw his handgun away so he wouldn't be tempted to just,
End it all, right there and then – take the bullet train right out of
this hell-hole,
Of mud and shit and Cholera . . .

He carved the heads of Demon's and Ghouls, maybe,
Perhaps to ward off terrible things, but what
could be more terrible than what he had seen, already?
So he planted those stakes around his campsite; more likely,
because he saw a Negro American soldier – carvin
things out of wood, and because they both enjoyed listening
        to Lena Horne and Ella Fitzgerald.
Soon he returned home from the war and met a woman.

Her name was Joyce.

This man was my grandfather...

AS IT BURNS

I dream only in black
Whole fields caught in flames
The slaves keep singing the same old song
The slaves keep dying the same old ways
With the needle
With the powder
With the pill
They tear their own eyes out of their sockets
I have learned to live with these dying visions now
Of the countless bodies charred
Left burning in the fields
In this bathroom where the tiles dripped blood
In this seclusion room they left my love raped . . .
In the bathroom where blood seeped into the drain-pipes
Moment to moment
Each body to fucking body
This hell we have tried to call existence . . .
It never seems to change . . .
Where women are raped like pigs
Each man dies his own slow death each day
Or where a man drinks himself to cancer
Or where newborn babies are left to rot
In some garbage bin or in some alley way
In this abortion city...
In this shithole where we are all eventually dying slow
You need to choose to live . . .

Slow or fast – the rhythm's break loose in my mind . . .
Children ripped from wounded sex holes
With coat hangers in subway toilets
Whores rotted with disease
I speak of a new form
Children without insect wings
Who will not, be forced to inhabit,
The rooming houses and alleyways of the State . . .
Where their forefathers lived before them . . .
Where we are all somebody's whore or somebody's abortion...
I will reignite this city in flames
I will burn these words into oblivion
Until the changes occur within this hardened soul . . .
Just give me a little beauty to smile at . . .
A crazy waitress in a ruined bar . . .
A mad bird singing on the edge of a cliff . . .
A life without the pain.

ANGEL HEART

- For Guzin

I spent three of the best years of my life,
fucked up, with insanity…
Doing time in seclusion rooms,
hospital hallways,
and smokers courtyards,
spitting on putrid food
which nursing staff brought me
through hospital trap-doors
while at night, I hallucinated,
the nightmares. . .
of the dripping blood
I witnessed rushing over me,
While I showered.

666 (Fuck The Disease)

Sweet virgin pussy is calling me (the disease)

I am a disease and my name is AID'S

I don't want pussy anymore, I don't want dick

I want to die, I hate being immortal

I want science to create a new A-Bomb, for me

And fuck me up, kill me, I hate being the agent of death

I hate God for where he has put me

I want to be music, not AID'S, I want to be love

I hate blood, I hate semen, I hate shit

I hate whores and the junkies and the queers who carry me

I hate the fucking Third World . . .

I hate that I am the virus of death . . .

I must be eradicated . . .

SOMETHING RAW

My city inhales its noise from a pair of
trapped gills. The sound of some sexy rhythm
moving in from the right. A saxophone player
dreaming of sly leopards in her sleep. Are you
one of these leopards?
Do you dream in logic?
Colour?
Is this you?
Do you live in here?

You need to learn to hear the sound of asphalt black
slipping away into ivory. Then understand this is all still nothing,
really at all. You see, I still remember you when you were
playing then chrome in 1985. Learning to ride on
subway trains
that switch from metal to electric blue.
This is what you gave me. Lead into gold.
And this poetic process makes liars and
cheats of us all.
I have said too much already.
Already, I have choked the thing
that was setting me free. I am sorry,
for this.

It's just that I am precise. Like Raymond Carver says, 'the words should
be precise, even if they are flat, they can still be powerful'.

My poetry is not beautiful. This *cheetah* is in the black and it had
to be that way

in order for you to be the ivory, which, is what you deserve, right
now

for what you have just given me. Keep reading and I will no
doubt

        fuck you up again.

Patti Smith playing *'Because The Night'*, and I can feel your

breasts like a veil to a beating heart, which beats

a menacing chaos. I had never meant to work the cycle like this.
Like a whore,

but isn't that what we are doing, sleeping

with words. Poetry. Isn't it a dirty art? Can't you see, that?

Something is happening here.

Through the trapped cages

of this bedroom's walls

I taste your soul in the beating noise

melting this ice which hangs on the memory,

of the cathedrals windows, in my mind. . .

still high. . . in this place -

so the ivory does not have to bleed the wax it

bleeds over the stripped whore

because it isn't capable of believing in the ability

to leave its cell

The pain of this image moving through us.

Like fear or true shortage of breath.

A tightened chest.

But for hell's sake
you
make all this pain stop
when you hold the silent note
that seems to stretch forever
in a second; or in a colour. . .
a sound
and when you give up logic and
reason
black and
white
to set this soul

free.

I SEE YOU

I see you
the woman with eyes of
the abyss.
The woman with cat-gut hair.
The woman who ties me to a wooden
chair and cuts my flesh
on the chest. You who watches me bleed, and kisses
me from where the blood runs…I see
you
the woman who drinks the sacred wine
in the cities of the dead night,
walking the acid rain beaches
of a child's
nightmare.
You who runs almost naked
through gardens
of the rich, drunk, high on wine,
high on
life.
You who swings from pain to
bliss; Heaven to Hell, who
doesn't understand
the logic
of a dream – yet,
still knows it,
feels it.

I see you.

Do you see me?

THE WAY SOME HAVE BEEN
FORCED TO SEE IT

I watch young children in my dreams
playing in their fields of Spanish vista's, wild
Mediterranean houses and drinking wine around a fire
yet, the vision is always interrupted by a darker logic
          that lives in shadows hovering over . . .
growing up without a real sense of love proving itself
but only then the knowledge enters
          of a fear beyond my years . . .

I notice the others dancing, singing, drinking liquor . . .
Their bonfires burning of neon and cheap insanity
Am I paying the price of learning too fast –

What it really means to be educated through a mental chaos?

This is the dream that can turn to nightmare too quickly
w/out beauty and w/out resonance
a storm shredding through the greenest of lands . . .
false death pumping genuine fear through
          thickened veins of the heart. . .
The death of a sickened timeless whore
          Immaculate, yet still stoned, regardless
& in the end it is all
just tired will and decay
and human cruelty

and all that they inflict upon us all . . .

by human dogs who believe they are at the top . . .

     When in fact they are all just fighting for a position in

     Their own form of a toxic hell . . .

     That burns bright under their decaying flesh

tell them a storm is coming

tell them to get the fuck out of their homes

tell them to leave and get the fuck out of the cold . . .

leave them cocked half-sure

in a world of bitterness and the taste of chrome . . .

push them all out into the streets and watch as all of them fall into
their own devised fucking madhouses of the street

Everything's eventually owned by the state

or somebody else, anyway. . .

Everything else is becoming clear now . . .

        clear as burning acid rain . . .

in slow motion liquid chrome . . .

dripping from the broken roof, upon whores

and junkies of the flesh . . .

tell them all that this is the love you are sending back

tell them all

in their fancy houses, front row church pews

each and every Sunday,

that this is what they are giving them in return,

for treason . . . as they swallow the fucking host –

of rusty stripped battery metal . . .

    Cooked up in hells kitchen.

What have they done to your feelings now
of love . . . the same the millions have felt it
each and every night
suffering in their bedrooms, boarding rooms,
        or motels above bars
        night cuts bone to ash
hold on because we are paving the way
        of a new dream, bursting eternal . . .
        A brand new schematic
making way for something
real, and making way for
purity
to be felt
after all this writing is over
I will return to a room
have a little money to get drunk on
and maybe play some nice
music . . . Coltrane, or Piaf
I know how you love that stuff
        Not those tortured voices that have been laid
            crimson in your head . . .

And love will not be ugly for us

            . . . when we finally sleep . . .

THE NIGHT I NEVER SLEPT

In the Dawn of the *Drawing of the Moon* . . .
fingers sharp like razors pointed, towards
the mildewed blackened holes . . .
As I laid there lysergic sick –
drifting *Across the Universe* . . .
And you played God . . .
When it wasn't like the ages past –
When you had to earn it – or when you had to fight for it . . .
as if Christ had been placed under your tongue

      yet, isn't it funny

      how the wafer always seems to cling to the back
of your throat . . . Sticky, like your fingers . . .

      As the mirror reflected a slanted image – the pain of
pissing blood . . . in a cell . . .

trains came into my desert station . . .

               . . . to station to station to station.
And in this night so blackened
Such a game of chess to you –
Nobody really ever knows where to run
When fear takes over . . .
If your ego wasn't so fierce, maybe you might not
Have tried to shift the gears
Towards my final winter –
But the seasons always shift themselves, anyway . . .
And it looked like it was going to be such a long,

      long ride . . .

All across the city and all *Across the Universe*
and into the rivers and the reddened sea's . . .

But finally . . . what made the stone
perspire . . . is the recognition –
    That you found pain . . .
Where I had already died

Years and years, before . . .

IN THE FLESH

Our lives
Devoid of meaning
Thinking of others while we fuck
Changing lanes
On highways or strips
made of neon
which has not yet stopped burning the false dreams
Of a poisoned mythology
snorting coke off bathroom
toilet seats
as well...
Too much cheap sex
In run down
motel rooms
Must try and glance beyond this lie
To a world with a reflective skin that shudders
To a place where children do not run scared
But play unthreatened in the sun
With mothers by their sides
Like a silky blue, early Picasso painting
Children kept inside safe fields
Not yet polluted by nightmares of oil
and a death like machinery
that lays flickering against the shadows of the night
as though it were a sick geometry that dances in death as it
steals it by the meter

must not get too lost in this search
For purity . . .
Laying down and around in the sickness
Begging for a grace, to move through me
And somewhere in-between these two extremes
I hang loose like a lost jazz musician
playing the mourning of his mother
I need to stop drinking and drifting
Alone
I got to keep from hanging tight
amongst the hundred metre
          crosses
that disarm men
in our religious wars
that dangle over our valleys
Like murder . . .
But where you and I dream of
          spotlights
as we awake

afraid.

But you aren't there, are you?
In a sense though
you are
you always are
under the frost of the headlights
under the sinking feeling of my loneliness

under the frosted pain
as I take another sip of my scotch whisky
and as I come out to dance in this sick world
in my own way
which is through the wasted poetry
performing a secret language
like that of an old silent movie
I forget the name of now

I sit ready for you
& your careful movement
But now I want something
Else
as well
lets try love
      Unconditional
Off-screen
      In the flesh
           For real
      This time.

CRAWLING AWAY

I turn my back as you stick the knife in
Then crawl away.
I will use my entire body to absorb your hatred,
It sinks into my filthy body, in its pores…like wet quicksand;
Caked with sticky blood.
Down on the shoreline of a scattered memory…
I still remember her eyes.
She never slipped away.
Even when you stuck the knife in;
Only slipped inside every now and then…
To give some kind of solace…
In those most brutal of nights…
When we were all alone.

THE TIGER IS MINE

They try and string me up
to torture this body. Hanging
inside a bucket of freezing water.
Sticking pins under my eyelids.
Ripping at my fingernails. Putting drugs
into my body, so they can fuck each
other, while I squirm in the dying fluids,

but I don't ever die.

A tiger bashes at my back to make
me write these words. I feel her iron claws
rip at my skin, deeper then deeper.
But they have already gotten me
used to the feeling. What the fuck?

Now, I kinda enjoy it.

WHAT IT TAKES

I have lived with insanity

for the majority of my life.

Been on and off the drinking,

when it has had to be numbed.

I am afraid, now to face it.

In the eyes.

It carves you up for each second you stare at it.

But you can learn to understand

its hunger

when you see starving as a gift.

Every good poet has starved in the fire,

every real artist

Frances Farmer, Bukowski,

Burroughs, Selby,

Hemmingway,

Hunter S. Thompson,

Jesus Christ, why

are the things of this nature so fucking hard to

fathom?

What is this trick?

Are you not meant to think about it.

Strap me to the gallows one last time,

I know how much you love to watch

the flesh slowly rot.

Do you think it stinks, like

rotten meat,

cooked in some second hand kitchen,
next to a whores motel
on Fifth Street.
Put an apple in the sick mouth of
insanity, and watch the whole fucking game
turn itself backwards, or on its
side. Give it a cross to give for recognition.
Is this what you are in the need of?
To notice my bleeding,
bleeding.
Bleeding, yes, it makes me want to run a mile.
When it starts to hurt like the sound of rust
scraping upon dirty steel.
I may as well give it up.
You will never understand where I am
coming from.
Just a starved, and naked,
shivering child
who doesn't understand his time
his place
or the math.

A good liar is just as important as a good
thief.

THE RAZORS EDGE

I have been marked
with the decision
trying to transform winter
into spring.

This I promise is what keeps us going. Breathing

breathing is good
when your swallowing
has become tedious.

I have began to notice change.
started to shift the gears
of a pale and folded movement

from mud to soft clay
stone into gold
shit into new matter

I have become the alchemist
stone magician and new performance artist
injecting my piss
into the bloody vein.

Where does it take us now.
Beyond the walls,

of stone and cold reason.

This I hope, will at least be freeing.

POEM FOR HUBERT SELBY, JR

You said throughout
your life, that you had started to die,
before you were born,
the small tubes stuck around your
tiny neck . . .
cutting off the air to your
newborn brain . . .
but you fought this,
with a pure rage -
even then,
and came out kicking and screaming
into the 20th Century . . .
This sometimes shitty
world . . .

Then you went into the Second World War as a marine on a ship.
And contracted bovine tuberculoses, from the cattle.
You fought this also, even though the doctor's and nurses
told you, you would probably never make it.
Fighting it as only you could, with
One whole lung collapsed and half of the other
Cut out, along with ten ribs, to go with it –
Which you asked to be made into letter openers
To give to your friends,
In Brooklyn.

Then came your realization.

That at sometime, you would die, 'really die . . .'

'not like it had been happening', all your life, 'nearly dying',

but you would, 'actually die' – and before you would die,

'two things would happen'. One – you would want to live,

 your life over – and two,

you would realize that you had done,

nothing with your life . . . This scared, the hell

out of you . . .

So you figured, 'I know the alphabet, maybe,

I could become a writer . . .'

And so you wrote . . .

And it saved your life, 'kept me alive,' you said . . .

And it saved mine also . . .

I WISH THAT I COULD WRITE
LIKE CHUCK PALAHNIUK

These hands which tore slow deformities
Off the face of our Christ, your Buddha
Left scars in the flesh that tried to print words
Off Burroughs' arsehole talking typewriter
Like Kerouac trapped in a cage, surrounded
By flies twice his normal size.

Am I left to
The wasted sound
Of John Cage . . .
        Playing silence.

I wish that could have been a Haiku, or this:
Trent Reznor the new God of New Orleans
With his new blue Gene   Zoe my queen
        Old S&M writing fetish fanzine
This should be printed on really tiny pulp sheets of paper
That can be licked and used as Lysergic Acid (25)
I want to be the new cult God that doesn't die young
Like Mr. Carroll, or Burroughs, or Bukowski
        These are my Gods.

        And it's hip to quote names of famous authors . . .
        If that's what'll get your arse sold . . .

We should started the beat generation a year earlier
In Vegas. And given it the right time to grow
Into mutual diseases like aids or cancer
That's the way we live, and you're right, we live in the shadow
Of the 1990's , where SHOTGUN size bullet holes
Form mansions in the heads of all our . . .

Heroes

A SCHOONER OF SCOTCH

Pulled the needle from his vein
Then he tried to gain a breath
Drank a schooner from his scotch
Woke up tasting death . . .

BUTCHER

I stare at them.

They're weak…

Like hanging corpses,

They walk around in bodies of flesh.

They're weak…

Look at them

Dead walking flesh.

Make's you feel special.

Mask of flesh wrapped around your face.

Will you kill again?

I'm a butcher.

I'm a butcher.

I'm the flesh man.

Watch me light my soul on fire…

Then dance around… In your skin.

I'm a butcher.

I'm a butcher.

I'm a flesh man.

I'm a butcher.

ABATTOIR

In the abattoir of the dead mans soul,
A soldiers projected memory plays against his marked eyelids,
Scarred by too much pain; scarred
From too much abuse, torment and mutilation,
War camps, where hostages bleed as bamboo punctures
      their decaying flesh, and limbs
Torn clean off their bodies, heads of the innocent,
      Severed by machete's . . . or axes.   .
A Japs sword stuck into his filthy tangled and warm intestines
      as he commits the one way train to death –
        by hari-kari.

A white screen w/the number eleven carved into it
Carved by blood . . .

Meat hangs from hooks in the doorways of the spaces
Between heaven and the many circles of hell.

Are these things meant to be a warning against the horror
The atrocities of the wars, good people fight in?

And we won't ever defeat this bullshit – it's an endless battle,
Pushing guts and blood and shit up hill . . .
The future generations are always scarred
By too much horror and that which came before . . .
We are all scarred by prominent death

And series of endless torments . . .

And is this all war is good for . . .

We have a series of endless nightmares now,
Inherited by our human waste of sin . . .

Eleven men on a wall ready to be shot down – their eyes,
Unable to see – due to the blackened hoods which,
Cover their fucking heads . . .

It's enough to make you sick.
The memories are bold and coated with slippery
Wet blood. And they form the shadow of torment
That this dead man, on trial – has held inside
Him, inside his mind for nearly all of his life . . .

The abattoir of the dead mans soul, memories live
In this place of mud and fear, and they're driven slowly
        Into exile – by the need for something else,
something pure.

Something to set me free from this world –
Could it be love?

Anything better than this pain, than this shit. . .

In this cell the blood drips from the walls . . .

Like it always has . . .

IN & OUT

I sit here tonight
with nothing
to do.
I've written three
stories
already.
They are probably going to need
a lot of editing and a lot of
reworking.
I'm onto the poems, now.
Needing to fill the idle
time.
When I am not working
I am trying to write
this stuff, &
searching, begging,
stealing
for a half decent line.
To one day make it at writing,
whatever this means.
To one day find a way out of this
second guessing,

maybe
not.

AT LEAST HUMAN

Some won't understand the logic
of melting churches
or bending clocks
                  & this is what fucked you up so long . . .
But all this time, understand, that as the others
swayed
you swayed to…

And this
at least makes you
human as well.

Doesn't it?

Maybe, more so . . .

WHITE ROOM

- For Jeremy

starving tigers
gnaw
at my flesh
while I remember
the feeling of insanity
naked fear
like the devil burning gasoline
across my naked flesh
my soul caught on fire
my body strung up and
tortured by hatred

the deadly snake
inflicting its venom
across my weeping wrists
while scars and bloody venom
bled into me as I tried
to wash and open up the veins . . .

I still remember the pain thoughout this shit
I was stuck in a seclusion room for two and a half weeks

It all appears now
like a snap-shot, of

occult photography

all those moments I pissed down the drain (& blood ran)

you noticed the fear within me
you saw what was capable

to turn shit into gold

basic alchemy . . .

now, I wear the pain and experience like armoured shield

the sound of the city
doesn't affect me like it use to

so long, I felt
too close to the silence
too far from the noise

growing up with the morning's disillusionment . . .

decay and debauchery . . .

I can remember these things well

from behind the thickened glass –
back when I was locked up in the public system

nurses watching me jerk hysterical in my own piss,
vomit, blood and come

they tried to analyze me
through hospital speaker phones

perhaps I was too afraid then
to heal from this shit . . .

it would take years, and I'm still evolving

for years I had been damaged
from too much booze, drugs
and too much self-abuse committed against
my own inner mind
mine was the soul debased

but I am trying to find grace and love . . .
amongst the brutality of life

I always use to fight against myself

when it was death's blackened leeches
when it was death's blackened parasites

for they all claimed to have the fucking cure

I couldn't cling to their remedies though

their schematic codes had been misplaced . . .
torn up . . . burnt, simply it was wasted paper now
they claimed to have it, anyway – the revised edition
        but fuck it . . .
it was no good to me anymore – even I knew that,
and I was outta there

I'd rather take my own time (years) to heal myself,
re-frame the shattered experience . . .

and finally I think I may be starting to heal now. . .

you were one of the good ones

who actually made a difference,
when I stood against people's trust
when I was concerned that I was just going to receive
another mental and physical

beating . . .

Thankyou.

MORNING GLORY

Morning rushed to greet you.

Piercing the light
that peels from your naked vein.
I think it beautiful the way day changes,
from light into new dawn.

I think it beautiful the way sharks...
                    decipher fear.

morning dances, your prelude was soft.
no more the thin lines of merchants to cut
your airways. you can breathe now.

Take this pain, for example
the way it leads to excess
                    will only cause you injury.

When in the end,
all you need is reversal from death's hold.

STARING DOWN THE BEAST

These demons crawling under my skin
Which taunt with baited breath.
Like a straight razor
On a new babies flesh.
Or a screaming child.
What does a man have to do?
To find peace in this world?
How much alcohol needs to be consumed
To shut out his own inner turmoil
And does it anyway?
Or only help to amplify your own screams to such
An inner pitch – that you feel like you are going to crack
From the insides out.

And how many of them do this to themselves,
night in – night out?
How many are the powders,
That they consume?
When will I find the woman who understands my life?
This thing inside of me,
Tries to dominate me.
But I will never give into it . . .

A place where the slanted silver mirrors,
        form bad shadow imagery, as I ride the electric subways,
and the nod works inside me – within the slumber, of a beautiful
        codeine dream . . . that stretches up and over me

until it becomes a codeine nightmare. . .
As well I realize, this is one of the bad trips. . .

No up, in this nightmare.

I see the beggars on the side of the underpass –
watching them move. . .

And I try to get it all down in one quick scrawl. . . as I go
close quarter with the beast – and the graffiti on
The concrete buildings; passing by as I sleep (on and off) . . .

In this train where I sit
and it almost seems like some surreal *Warner Brothers*,
cartoon animation. . .

I wonder how my brother is going with his paintings. . .
Always did like to draw?

Suddenly the train stops;
it's time to get off. . .

But I don't.

Some trips last a lifetime.

33

Will you put it?
into boxes, or jars
underneath your hallway.

Where do you place
the things you keep sacred.

I know this madness
isn't that important,

but it is what I do.

TONGUE TO THE RAIL

Tongue to the rail this night
With all matter of things passing. The chaos sets in
moves outside the patterns.

This lizard half awakened on dust feels only
half as vicious now
      as this stone begins to sink.

        A shower in blood, chrome tiles, the whole motel
room destroyed.
        Christ has his crucifixion day – and you will have
your choice. Your will . . .

What you inherit will inherit you:

        The cold breeze whips at my naked spine
        as she dries my feet
        with her wet jet-black hair.

        chrome frozen dream sprays you
        sometimes . . .

(If only that were the way it was…)

    Let me tell you how it wasn't:

      Couples walking naked, hand in hand,

Flowers in their hair, singing songs of Love,
And peace. . .

Through desert highways
lightning striking down their power line souls
as the clown laughed inside my mind . . .

things were simply: Lucid.

Tongue to the rail tonight.

All mirrors reversed themselves,

              And the night stabbed my side with
somatic nightmares

       Technicolor blindness set in . . .
       Soon to be replaced by a bleached out
version . . .

       Like:

              Trees. Loneliness.
Diamonds of blood . . .
              Rest. Nothing at all.

       In. Out. In. Out.

       Peace/Pain.

Tomorrow Is Your New Day.

A MAN IN RUINS

You walk through fields
Of hollow nightmares
And this is your mind
This is your scarred burning mind…
There used to be a time when you were clean
There used to be a time when you wanted something pure
A little more real . . .
And you would've fought for it –
A dead body clinging to the blood wet sheets
An apartment of a dead man's world
Soaked in shit
Soaked in months of pissed out urine
You are a collector of the body images
This is all you have left after the rot
When all has been said and done
What will you be?
Will you be the only one dying by the side of the railway track
alone with some needle in your vein. Or will you be something
else apart from this?
I pour these words out
Afraid of change
But it is the best I can do . . .
Somebody marked by insanity
The threat of self-immolation.
I will find a meaning through the madness.
I will find purity within.

UNTITLED #1

Her ankles slit, like cut flowers
a young child's Encyclopedia. Purity sustaining
itself. Through the justified logic we had earned through sickness

The night was long. The morning, even longer
twelve hours, the night, the storm didn't stop.

These words never meant too much. Train boards the platform,
"so long – flat-foot," word's cut from an age old memory,
lost in your youth.

Needles like harpoons, on beaches where couples, fuck,
Or lose sight in the abattoirs, or next to a train stop
at the end of the line . . . And you can't ever let these things
just end there. For the memory just jolts like quickened lightning,
Forever . . . You hang there, like dead meat . . .
You pay always, for these things you earn.

COMING DOWN

You found floating boats like chess-piece horses,
in your bloodstream. And got wasted there, in your nod.
I wish you could sleep forever in your perfect dreams. Nod's.
Black eye-shadow, forged like cinema drapes, Horses, with a
capital H.

You found wild orchids clinging to your veins
Like the backs of your eyelids.

The pin-prick's were harsh and unrelenting.
In your dome of summer and scar.
The booze flowed forever there . . .
A brown cardigan, lost on ward fourteen,
Split screen, De Palma logic . . . I will take you there,
Like a raft in my used blotter bloodstream . . .
Like a canoe through to death . . . and beyond.
Be careful of the jaundice I have left over from birth . . .
Cocaine leopards sit in dream chairs, and booze, flows eternal,
Those were good but older days.
Hanging to a rope suspended over chair . . . As I roll cigarettes
and wait for my ethereal freedoms of memory to catch up
And it comes in fragments . . . now and then –
the pain . . . now and again . . .
the memories, the confusion of what is real,
what is dream . . . what is nightmare and so it goes on . . .

with sharp breaks of graceful nostalgia . . . like waves . . .

Cutting through our sleep . . .

. . . blonde hair & blue eyes . . .

Who gives a fuck, anymore?
As I return from whatever high I've been on.

I wish it could have been you.

Always, coming down . . . always coming down . . . always
coming . . . down . . . always . . .

MADNESS

The sewn edges
of your winter attire
help to build the scars
that encapsulate
madness.

I know this only
because I speak in terms
of madness.

And this madness
which I believe,
speaks in terms
of us.

Comes only
from a form of
repetition,
that in itself is
mad.

SEASONS OF MEMORY

I want the winter fate, with
its reasons undefiled. And summer
twisted with new variation.

Everything at once . . .

Like children dancing through
ancient playgrounds, across
their cities. At night they carved
images of violence, into
their veins.

I want my seasons purity.
I think I am deserving of this.

WHITE WALLS

Your white skin immersed
deserts of soft rain desecrated.
Some wisdom is only selected
by ancient words, and of a time
less pure. Two lives separated
by a simple car parking lot, and
a man who collects pads in the
same ways that I do. Ironic eyes
are lost to the begging of year old
children, when they can only see at
close range.

Now my fingers stroke at madness.
And to those men who walked pure
in their own diseases, I waited for a
rain less tortured. And to see his blue light
flashing which it finally did in my
own unique way. On the way to some
fucking road trip…

I found my way through waters of disillusionment.
As I found myself on the verge of being dead.

HORSES FOR DREAMS

We were with you when you wore
Black down the isles of New York City
When each tear pummelled the stars.

        And the children fell through
        the fields like stallions.

That life could be somehow precious
I suppose it could.

Dreams left scattered

    and you are still singing
    with full lips   (your dress faded).

Legs strangling the many small
    actresses of the world . . .

UNTITLED #2

When in the presence of beauty
I always look back at something putrid
This is the catholic guilt I have inherited
From years, swallowing the host, that burnt
Inside my mouth.
      I am lonely here:
Where trees make no sense
      but taunt like childhood laughter
where the river always runs too fast
backwards

I am in the process of reclaiming a vision
That took me years to perfect . . .
From opiates and the bad nutrition, of soaked paper
While standing in the isles of a dilapidated church w/a girl,
Stripping me out of reality . . .

And the processions take place. As I waited, out ethereal
Freedoms. I paid for years earlier, written down
On blood-soaked paper.

THE PRICE OF ADMISSION

These walls seem scarred by a generation
that sprayed profanities
on cold granite walls, set in blood
by the suffering of those who knew their passion and loss.
Memory. What have you done with this now?

      Have you lit it up on fire?

Against the moss which grows slow
on a fingernail that scratched at a pair of chrome
teeth. Like smokers stains. Cancer, burnt a hole in love.
The sun is always blotted out for us, you fucking know what I
mean . . . as I am forced at gun point – to listen once more to
The Darkest Sides of The Moon.

Are you slowly becoming ruined by poisoned youth; or
Swallowed up in a mythology which seems too large? –

Was your reality set to be devoured, and a
calculated attempt of directed hatred?

Locked up in their jars like trapped, bugs. Like a bleeding
watercolor, stolen from one more ancient gallery.
Listening to the phonograph when
none of this even mattered –
or was even worth the price of admission;
this shit isn't even worth the bloody pulp it's printed on . . .

And it is bloody –

A stuffed nose begins to bleed . . . and my temples hurt.

I don't really know about this shit anymore…

HORSES

I give you horses,
dreams to incite madness,
and a lifetimes worth of moments
to throw in the fire. I give
you this because you asked it of me.

I know there must be
a catch…

So you stuck out your arm to incite madness…

Death. Death. Death.

The face of Jesus forever stuck
in my mind. Repetition.

Horses moving through a glassy tube with floating
crimson blood.

Horses.

Repetition.

Life on a dime coin . . .

ROOM 6

She gives me word on paper.

Which states and forecloses
a growing network
                of new world order.

I lost my ears to the sound…
        of knives sharpening over malicious
                playgrounds.

In which you showed me the guidelines.

And I'm glad that I
                pissed all over their
                        food.

For the hallways wore endless variations
and only shy piano music would break their
walls.

THE BIRTH OF A FROZEN MEMORY

-For Joyce and Leo Fatouros

You once found secret armies
whose tortures had silenced you.

But no more . . .

And at once you were pure.
With hands untainted by cold fractured skin,
that laid damage on hot steel.

There was always memory.
Worked inside . . .

You taught me faith.
You taught me trust.
You taught me love . . .

And at this moment of brilliance
When chambers of madness are slowly released . . .
Something more pure comes from all this –
It finally makes sense . . .
The things you had been teaching me, all these years . . .
You provided me the anti-venom to a pain,
I had to heal from the inside
I found a sense of purity and grace and found my worth there…
When I'd returned from the years of drug abuse and drinking
once more, but with a purpose and design, now

Without the persistence of demise.

You taught me one more thing that I could never have imagined
But that is yet, to sail . . .

REASONS TO LEAVE

-Sandoz

I once saw everything as a simple gesture of fate.

Two hollow motions at the closed
gates of infinity. Opened up for a moment
to see my grace defiled. As I grazed
at life untainted.

It was your body holding out on reason –
on diligence. As I created signs to keep us
pure. At a moments distance.

I spoke only of clarity…

Am I guilty of this?

RESISTANCE

- For Gerard And Madeline Sier

I held you near
as your moment fell close
and at that same time
pierced all eternity

Your body was still warm
From the vapours,
In which your flesh had left behind -
Its silent bite

A soft, death of the physical world, which
Time emancipates

It is hidden
In each gallery
A slower method
To define madness

By these laws
I have chosen to define
And ultimately found
Resistance

THE BLEACH BURNS MY EYES

as it burns out the images of
desperate whores, filled with syphilitic cocks
and enough hatred to fill
a civil war death camp.

scarred virgins… blood-letting in blood-crystal sands
useless images
that would cling to your mind
and try to destroy your sense of self
while trying to attain a sense of my own meaning
and purity. There are shadows lined inside my
soul . . . like bubbles, in an hour glass, I wanted to brake open.

And fuck how I wish I could make
somebody see underneath this flesh
that it's not all
      useless hatred &
      excess.

      That there is some purity and empathy.
      Perhaps even love . . .

I wish somebody could see like I do, the visions
haunting my soul, which begin to set me
on fire each night like a young man building a life
carved out of delayed suicide –waste –

living through all these feelings -
while somewhere else a young woman
        is getting raped and is left bleeding on the side of
a railway track…this is not real, but fuck it feels real enough.
While this poem, is starting to read you…I know
its being built inside my mind, and sometimes...
you wonder why you keep going through with
all the same old shit .

Useless excess…
that I wish I could contain
and just at least feel a little worth
to rid myself of this decayed stench
of soul sweat and death… Like
rotting chicken in a bowel of shit.
Humans hang in this seclusion room from iron
hooks in my minds eye…
And maybe this is sickening poetry
However, I make no excuse for it
The words that work themselves through me….

Don't expect me to die, begging
for a mercy
that I know
will not come…

        I have died many times before and I will no doubt again.
The same thing over and over…

Life. Death.

And taxes…

THE WAY OF THE WORD

There is blood on the pages
of all the great books.
Do you know how they suffer?
For the line.
It is the only way
to make it count.
When it is all over
if you are not
shivering
and totally alive
light shining
upon you,
yet, feeling more vulnerable than ever,
made to feel weak from the expression of the word,
ready to be filled up again
then you have not
given anything
of yourself to the art of the

word.

TIME

Time changes your season, and it is too late to conspire
against new threats – that endanger the moving truth
I have come through time and there is that word again
A word, which governs our lives…

TIME.

    Small Fragment:
I see a man sitting on a train,
He's reading a small magazine,
The magazine he is reading
Is called TIME.

UNTITLED #3

They have kept you here, your
secret attics of stored frozen sunlight.
Stripping away the boundaries
that trapped your winter.

I am still here,
in your soft resistance,
where it is morning.

marvellous how light lays scattered over cities of ruin

(where in an instant I am gone)

like worn out blood keeps my eyelids polished, or
drained   regions of new soldiers invading
    their month
      brought back home from torture.

"How we tried to speak of inquisitions."

When this is your fate. Howling vessels of bookshelf truths,
trees left with inverted shadows . . .

And it's here that life pervades itself . . .

But it's here I make a stand.

WINTERS DREAM

I wait in a reclusive silence,
for the light of a sun that never seems to arrive.

        I know the reason I am
    here,
        drifting
            amongst the reeds -
of this poisoned river,
      which rushes like blood from a virgin suicide
      towards a city that never sleeps; towards a city
        always travelling South
        always sleeping in the dirt.

        This city is a place where young children play
in a playground, marked
by rusty beer cans and dirty syringes, pills and
        used condoms, razor blade's and knive's
sharpened from
        the first kill or self-mutilation

        This place where the young children
are driven to watch their ultimate
      dreams fall empty – if they're not careful
        forced to watch their own ultimate demise,

        always coming down –

If they can't change the paths they're on . . .

Where we spent our wasted youth
    almost twelve years of our lives resting against cold
granite, cell walls

    where we got lost
    to the endless night
    and stored a chamber of darkness without time

    in a city where we almost drove ourselves insane . . .
    Day in – night out . . .

(some making it all the way)

        . . . then I flash to the images of business women, in
power-suits
    walking in total nonchalance . . .
sex fantasies playing themselves out on the subway platforms,
for the perverts
    jerking themselves hysterical on the steel trains,
    moving quickly
to dry their cocks between newspaper pages sticky and filthy
and to wipe the off-white seed . . . with drug-addled fingers that
swipe the shit away . . .

    . . . whores, pushers, pimps
    children of the locust . . .

always marked for death.

theirs is the longest of winters

awaiting the slow tortures of pain to be over,
                    through cold granite cell walls
the relentless winter
moves in and out of time   as we shivered

on dirty mattresses soaked in our own urine . . .

        . . . in some seclusion room . . .

laying waste to the freezing cold mattresses
of hospital beds we would piss on
                            where we washed ourselves
with blood – to clean, as they watched   us go mad with our
own diseases, and the bipolar river's had almost

drowned us back then . . .

        but we sweated it out   (with slow death in silence)

        awaiting the changes to occur
        that we thought would never

        come . . .

But maybe they have now.

POEM FOR A DRIFTER

Bending bodies float past steel rivers,

> where in this world everything lays reversed –
turned as it were

> and one's opposite becomes one's truth
(black water fills my canoe).

Then suddenly you are alone in your bedroom.

> Trembling, yet understanding in
> life it is alright

> to tremor.

> When Fear isolates you from

> Love.

> And love is just another word: and
> it exists without debt.

> or so you might

> IMAGINE.

> Imagine too, is just a word . . .

Does the water make you feel cold. And does it seem as though you are standing in the corroding acid rain of hell . . .

> Does Euphoria not work as a Euphemism for you.

> Do I sound like I am isolating,

> myself.

Then this will have been of all worth

if you just comprehend

these are just

words

without debt…

POEM FOR RIMBAUD

I wiped the chrome tears off Rimbaud's face
while he stood burning at the foot of their crucifix,
that which we were afraid to inherit
became our worst fear harbored.

I am his loyal scapegoat.
His fucking animal masochist.
The lamb of God.
I am his experimentation gone bad.
The orange they should have cast away at birth.
The man they tried to censor.

Lights flickered in the hallways,
as she swallowed moths from the cotton lampshades
and painted fingernails black to die.
And God's coloured words peeling back the thick of their flesh:
Words sounded:
          "Justice is pitched when the mirror is broken…"

SECLUSION ROOM

I will trace the edge of their needle (it will enter with force)
    And might lull me with the taste of an addicts pain.
        Am I fulfilling my role in the play,
           of their theatre of cruelty . . .

        Do you notice the way I write this: like a pattern
        the way junkies are meticulous about their
        diseases.

This is a disease: my writing, this thought process. I want to be
like a God:

"Sun go up, sun go down, you will do what you're told…"

    The sun dies and goes to heaven.
        The plants all loved him but they'll go on.

See the shit you write when you are locked in a green room.
Believing it is *Heaven* when *Hell* told you otherwise.

           I am a recluse now

           I lick the flowers off the walls

           They all taste like acid

           And you know that metal, chrome
           biting taste you get from LSD
           (blotter paper)

           In your mouth…

Look at me: here. the nurses all look like *devils*.

fuck 'em.

(they won't let me out)

END OF THE NIGHT

I walked the road to the end of the highway
Found something was going on there . . .
Didn't quite know what it was
Or where it came from . . .
Dripping blood . . . cut-open animals . . . dead birds –
Dead lamb . . .
Found circus clowns on seeping stilts.
Melting vaginas and unreliable watches . . .
Found babies wearing gas masks made in Germany.

Let it ride . . .
Watch it flow . . .

You kept going,
Until there was no place left to explore . . .
Top of the mountain side.
The face of Jesus in your mind.
And ice bubbles running up and down your crooked spine . . .

Bad nutrition.

BRUTAL NIGHT

In the most brutal of nights
My heart pumped battery acid
And my dreams were inverted . . .

The red sea flooded my bedroom, its walls were an
Epiphany of rain dripping down from the ceiling
And smashing against the windowpanes . . .

The radiator was loud, broken
As I tried to play a fractured guitar . . .

My father made me coffee . . .
As I watched a film
About an innocent man, locked up to die
Whose initials were:

J.C.

LAST WORDS

their (children)
some interesting
try to find, the ways
of senselessness

this coupled
with despair
and the loss of nations
helps to form
apathy

EPIPHANY

- For Jess

I've been around,
seen some things;
walked through piss soaked hallways
as I waited for my mind to catch up
with the hell of my experience . . .
the torments of the public and private hospital's
I have spent time in . . .
And while the private hospital's were never
nearly as bad
as the public one's
they still had they're
downfalls.
And trust me;
      trust is important –
for most people never see it . . . clearly;
while they constantly abuse it . . .
their positions in life . . .
You probably already understand,
What it is I am trying to say.

And who am I to assume things about you?
For I hardly know you . . .

A lot of things have gone on through the years –
towards keeping me down . . .

. . . *fucked* up . . . perhaps you are like this also . . .

Maybe not –I hope not –

I hope your journey is good,

At least from this point forwards . . .

   Folded paper and painted canvas . . .

   I am guilty, of imagining;

How your blue eyes may be excited – *physically*;

as they are scanning over the word *fuck* . . . in my poetry . . .

   When I feel you are more used to reading

     Jane Austin in a psych ward; and imagining this
concept . . .

this idea,

how things work through the countless cycles . . .

In nuthouses . . .

where agony,

and pain, and

    . . . insanity . . . and sometimes torture . . .

Are linked by experience

In these places – paper means everything.

I just wanted to say,

Thank you.

THE LAST POEM

The streets have left you, thinking

There is no place else to go, but

Inside yourself, to a place, filled with fear,

Self-doubt, contemplation of the great

Destroyer, the abyss, the mirror of your nightmares.

Are you afraid of the laughing

Demon, that burns inside your soul?

Are you afraid of the black river,

Never seen?

Are you afraid of the graceless women?

Is this the last poem?

Is this the last straight branch, carrying the last dead body

Of the last good soldier?

Are you afraid to look in the shadows?

Will you live again?

Do you hold the seeds of love?

www.ingramcontent.com/pod-product-compliance
Lightning Source LLC
Chambersburg PA
CBHW020513100426
42813CB00030B/3231/J